Dear Parent:
Your child's love of reading starts here!

Every child learns to read in a different way and at his or her own speed. Some go back and forth between reading levels and read favorite books again and again. Others read through each level in order. You can help your young reader improve and become more confident by encouraging his or her own interests and abilities. From books your child reads with you to the first books he or she reads alone, there are I Can Read Books for every stage of reading:

SHARED READING
Basic language, word repetition, and whimsical illustrations, ideal for sharing with your emergent reader

BEGINNING READING
Short sentences, familiar words, and simple concepts for children eager to read on their own

READING WITH HELP
Engaging stories, longer sentences, and language play for developing readers

READING ALONE
Complex plots, challenging vocabulary, and high-interest topics for the independent reader

ADVANCED READING
Short paragraphs, chapters, and exciting themes for the perfect bridge to chapter books

I Can Read Books have introduced children to the joy of reading since 1957. Featuring award-winning authors and illustrators and a fabulous cast of beloved characters, I Can Read Books set the standard for beginning readers.

A lifetime of discovery begins with the magical words "I Can Read!"

Visit www.icanread.com for information
on enriching your child's reading experience.

I Can Read Book® is a trademark of HarperCollins Publishers.

Library of Congress Control Number: 2014958851
ISBN 978-0-06-230386-8 (trade bdg.) — ISBN 978-0-06-230385-1 (pbk.)

18 19 SCP 10 9 8 7 6 ❖ First Edition

I Can Read!

SHARED My First READING

Pete the Cat's TRAIN TRIP

by James Dean

HARPER

An Imprint of HarperCollinsPublishers

Pete the Cat is going

to visit his grandma.

He gets to ride on a train!

Pete's mom buys three tickets.

She gives one to Pete

and one to his brother, Bob.

Pete looks up at the big board.

"Our train is leaving at

ten o'clock," he says.

A train speeds by.

"That's a cargo train,"

Bob tells Pete.

Pete's train has arrived.

"All aboard!"

calls the conductor.

Pete's mom finds three seats.

"I can't wait to see Grandma,"

says Bob.

"I can't wait to explore

the train!" says Pete.

The conductor comes
to collect the tickets.
Pete hands over his.

"I love trains," says Pete.

"I'll show you around,"

says the conductor.

Pete follows the conductor
from car to car as the floor
rumbles under his feet.

"Wow!" Pete says when they
get to the caboose.

"We're going over a bridge."

14

Pete sees his mom and Bob.

They are at the snack bar!

"I got this for you," says Bob.

Pete follows the conductor.

He goes to the front of the train.

"Come in!" says the engineer.

19

"Wow!" Pete says.

The engineer shows him

the engine.

The engineer shows Pete

the train's brakes.

There is a tunnel up ahead!

As they go through the tunnel,

Pete gets to honk the horn.

Toot! Toot!

Everything is light again!

"Thanks for showing

me around," Pete says.

On his way back to his seat,
Pete stops and makes
new friends.

They live in different towns.

They are getting off

at different stops.

Pete plays games.

A little kid wears his hat.

Pete sings a song.

What a groovy ride!

"We get off at the next stop,"

says Pete's mom.

Toot! Toot!

Pete looks out the window

and sees . . .

29

"Grandma!"

Pete is the first one
off the train.

Pete's grandma gives him
a big hug.
It feels good.

31

Pete loves riding the train.
But he loves his grandma
even more!